THE WORLD BANKERS AND THE DESTRUCTION OF AMERICA

Major (Ret.) James F. Linzey

LINZEY PUBLISHING HOUSE

THE WORLD BANKERS
AND THE DESTRUCTION OF AMERICA
Major (Ret.) James F. Linzey

Cover Design by Istvan Szabo, Ifj.
http://www.sapphireguardian.com

Printed in the United States of America
ISBN 978-1-936857-19-7

Linzey Publishing House
P.O. Box 300366
Escondido, California

OTHER BOOKS BY JAMES F. LINZEY

A Divine Appointment in Washington, DC
Baptism in the Spirit
The Holy Spirit
Moral Leadership
Why the Conservative Mind Matters
(Contributing author)

PREFACE

In November 1985, I was given a direct commission into the United States Air Force Reserves as a chaplain with the rank of first lieutenant. At the same time I was a schoolteacher in the Los Angeles Unified School District. I was in Watts not far from the horrifying beating of Reginald Denny, which was the beginning of severe rioting and looting. I was, in fact, driving out of Watts as that occurred, as quickly as I was allowed to drive by law, on my way to an event I had planned at Norton AFB in San Bernardino, California.

For several years up to that time, I had a surreal feeling that what I saw in society was not as it seemed to be. I could not pinpoint what I sensed, but it seemed like there was a subversive spirit undermining American society. Yet I could not substantiate it. No one told me this. I did not know what to do with what I sensed. So I began asking questions in the military to individuals only if I learned that they knew something I did not know, and if I felt safe to ask. Much to my amazement, I began learning things I did not know, which substantiated my discernment that something was dreadfully wrong in America.

The Dream

In January of 1987, I dreamed that I was in a concentration camp for Christians. I was in an area fenced in with a chain link fence that had barbed wire on top. The area seemed rectangular, front to back. Other Christians were in there with me. I don't know how many were there, but I remember seeing about a dozen or more people. We could not see the sky. For some reason it was not visible inside the compound. Perhaps the lack of a sky symbolized darkness. In front were some American soldiers. Suddenly they began mowing us down with automatic weapons. I found myself grabbing for metal folding chairs I had not previously seen, and, with others, I began shielding myself from the bullets. After a while it stopped.

From out of nowhere, Christians rushed to the front left corner of the compound in a panic and tried to climb over the fence. They failed to get over. Then they rushed to the front right corner and succeeded at getting over to escape the hellish nightmare. I joined them as fast as I could. As soon as I climbed over into freedom, I could see the clear blue sky.

Just then, as quick as we were free, I saw in the sky that they were coming for us. Helicopters were flying our way. We looked for a place to hide, but there was no place to go. The only object near us was a set of bleachers. And that was no place to hide, though some tried. We were again about to be arrested. Suddenly I woke up, startled.

Since then, I've had three more dreams similar to this one. The two following dreams were also in 1987. The fourth dream was in 2010.

The Role of America

Historically, the role of any nation's Armed Forces has been to secure its nation's borders, shores and airspace. But the United States is failing on all three fronts.

Historically, the role of any nation's government has been to establish and adhere to sound monetary policies. But the United States is spending itself purposely into oblivion, and it is being "told" what its policies will be and that she must adhere to them.

And, historically, the role of peace-loving nations has been to respect the sovereignty of all other nations and to attend to their own internal affairs. But the United States is too involved in the affairs of other nations, and it has allowed other nations to become too involved in the inner workings of the United States.

The contents of this book was originally prepared as a speech, prepared by my former college English professor who assisted me in the research and the writing. I am not an expert in the subject matter, but I sensed a "Call to Duty" to come to my country's aid to do my part to save her as any respectable human being would do, and as every minister of the Gospel is called to do, and to prevent what I saw in dreams from becoming a reality.

DEDICATION

*To The United States pastors who have the
biblical obligation to lead their communities to uphold
the United States Constitution and to preserve life, liberty
and the pursuit of happiness*

CONTENTS

CHAPTER 1:
NATIONAL DEBT
AND MONEY SUPPLY

Statistics

Here are some startling statistics.

- In 1901, the national debt of the United States was less than $1 billion. It stayed at less than $1 billion until we got into World War I. Then it jumped to $25 billion.
- The national debt nearly doubled between World War I and World War II, increasing from $25 to $49 billion.
- Between 1942 and 1952, the debt zoomed from $72 billion to $265 billion.
- In 1962, it was $303 billion.
- By 1970, the debt had increased to $383 billion.
- Between 1971 and 1976 (only 5 years) it rose from $409 billion to $631 billion.
- The debt experienced its greatest growth during the 1980s, fueled by an unprecedented peacetime military buildup. In 1998, the outstanding public debt soared past $5.5 trillion.

The "share" of this debt for every man, woman and child is currently over $21,000 and will continue to increase at an average of $630 million every day (and this doesn't include the $26 trillion in individual credit card debts, mortgages, automobile leases, etc.).

In 1900, the average American worker paid few taxes and had little debt. Last year payments on debts and taxes took more than half of what he earned.

Our debt is Spiraling:
- In 1910, the U.S. federal debt was only $1 billion, or $12.40 per citizen.
- By 1920, after only six years of Federal Reserve, the federal debt was $24 billion, or $228 per person.
- In 1960, the federal debt reached $284 billion or $1,575 per citizen.
- In 1998 the federal debt passed $5.5 trillion, or $20,403.90 per person (each man, woman, child).

If the present trend continues, we can expect the national debt to nearly double again within the next six to eight years. By then the interest on the debt alone should be in the $400 billion a year range.

Today we stand before the dawn of a New World Order. Most of the revenue collected by the federal government in the form of individual income taxes will go straight to paying the interest on the debt. At the rate the debt is increasing, eventually we will reach a point where, even if the government takes every penny of its citizens' income via taxation, it will still not collect enough to keep up with the interest payments.

The government will own nothing. The people will own nothing. The banks will own everything.

An adequate supply of money is indispensable to a civilized society. People can get along without many things, but without money nothing would be the same:
- all industry would stop,
- farms would become only self-sustaining units,
- surplus food would disappear,
- jobs requiring the work of more than one man would

16

remain undone,
- shipping and large movement of goods would stop,
- hungry people would plunder and kill to remain alive, and
- all government except family would cease to function.

In 1930, America did not lack industrial capacity, fertile farmlands and skilled and willing workers. It had an extensive and efficient transportation system in railroads, road networks and waterways. Communications between regions and localities were the best in the world, with telephone, teletype, radio and a government mail system. In the 1930s, the U.S. lacked only one thing: an adequate supply of money to carry on trade and commerce.

In the 1930s, the bankers, the only source of new money and credit, deliberately refused loans to industries, stores and farms. They required payments on existing loans, and money rapidly disappeared from circulation. Goods were available for purchase, and jobs were waiting to be done, but lack of money brought the nation to a standstill.

Thus the United States of America was put in a "depression" and bankers took possession of hundreds of thousands of farms, homes and business properties. The people were told that times are hard and money is short. Those excuses were not enough to account for the thousands of people who were robbed of their life savings and property to pay off the banks.

World War II ended the depression. The same bankers who had no loans for peacetime houses, food and clothing suddenly had unlimited billions to lend for army barracks and uniforms. With the sudden increase in money, people were hired, farms sold their produce, factories went to two shifts, and mines reopened. The

Depression was over. Many things are blamed for causing the Depression, but the truth is that the lack of money brought it, and adequate money ended it.

When we can see the disastrous results of an artificially created shortage of money, we can better understand why our Founding Fathers insisted on placing the power to "create" money and the power to control it ONLY in the hands of the Federal Congress.

The Founding Fathers believed that all citizens should share in the profits of the country, and therefore the federal government must be the only creator of money. Since the Federal Congress was the only legislative body subject to all the citizens at the ballot box, the Congress was the only safe depository of so much profit and power. The Founding Fathers wrote out simply, "Congress shall have the power to Coin Money and Regulate the Value Thereof."

Federal Reserve Board

Prior to 1913, America had been a prosperous, powerful nation. But in December of 1913, Congress passed what has since been known as the Federal Reserve Act. It simply authorized the establishment of a Federal Reserve Corporation, run by a Board of Directors (The Federal Reserve Board). The act divided the United States into twelve Federal Reserve "Districts." This law completely removed from Congress the right to "create" money or to have any control over its creation, and it gave those functions to the Federal Reserve Corporation. The propaganda claimed that this act would "remove money from politics" and prevent "boom and bust" economic activity from hurting our citizens.

The people were not told, and most still do not know, that the Federal Reserve Corporation is a private corporation controlled by bankers and therefore is operated for the financial gain of the bankers rather than for the good of the people. The creation of the IRS and personal Federal Income Tax occurred in the same year that the Federal Reserve Act was passed into law. The IRS was set up so that the government could repay its debt to the bankers via taxing the wealth of the common people (Griffin, 3).

How did the United States come to be controlled by economic interests? Griffin's premise is that, historically the only means by which a government has ever been able to "secure the subordination of citizens to the state" is war. War is used to make the masses put up with all kinds of privation, taxation and controls without complaint (Griffin, 2). Open war may not work, but there are several forms of war. The typical war system may have to be replaced because "it may not be possible to create a world government in which all nations will be disarmed and disciplined by a world army—a condition we call 'peace'" (Griffin, 2). Notice, though, that there are other ways to control a people.

History shows us that nations can be conquered by one of three methods.

1. Conquest by war. This method usually fails because the captives hate the captors and rise up and drive them out. Much force is needed to maintain control, making it expensive for the conquering nation.
2. Conquest by religion. Men are convinced they must give their captors part of their earnings as "obedience to God." Such captivity is vulnerable to philosophical exposure or to overthrow by armed force, since religion by its nature lacks military force to regain control.
3. Conquest by economics. This takes place when nations are placed under "tribute" without the use of visible force or coercion. The victims do not realize they have been conquered. "Tribute" is collected

from them in the form of "legal" debts and taxes, and they believe they are paying it for their own good or to protect them from some enemy. Their captors become their benefactors and protectors.

Though number 3 is the slowest conquest to impose, it is often quite long lasting because the captives do not see any military force against them, and their religion is left more or less intact. They have freedom to speak and travel, and they participate in elections for their rulers. They do not realize they are conquered and that the instruments of their own society are used to transfer their wealth to their captors.

The Federal Reserve System uses the methods of conquest by economic situations.

Most people believe that the Federal Reserve Bank is a branch of the U.S. Government. It is not. The Federal Reserve Bank is a private company. Today the Federal Reserve controls and profits by printing money, through the Treasury, regulating its value. The interest on that money is collected by the Federal Reserve (not by our government) and gives us the National Debt.

The Federal Reserve banking system collects billions of dollars in interest annually and distributes the profits to its shareholders. The Congress gave the Federal Reserve the right to print money through the Treasury at no interest to the Federal Reserve. The Federal Reserve creates money from nothing and loans it back to us through banks, and it charges interest on our currency. The Federal Reserve also buys government debt with money printed on a printing press and charges U.S. taxpayers interest on that money.

If the government runs a deficit, the Federal Reserve prints dollars through the U.S. Treasury and buys the debt, and the dollars are circulated into the economy. In 1992, taxpayers paid the Federal Reserve banking system

$286 billion in interest on debt the Federal Reserve purchased by printing money virtually cost free. Forty percent of our personal federal income taxes goes to pay this interest. The Federal Reserve's books are not open to the public. Congress has yet to audit it (see "The Federal Reserve Fraud,"
http.//www.biblebelievers.org.au/moneymad.htm, 1).

The Federal Reserve Board and the Federal Reserve banks acting together are private credit monopolies. No body of men is more entrenched in power than the arrogant credit monopoly that operates the Federal Reserve Board and the Federal Reserve banks ("Fed...Fraud," 1).

Our people's money, to the extent of $1,200,000,000, has within the last few years been shipped abroad to redeem Federal Reserve Notes and to pay other debts. The greater part of our monetary stock has been shipped to foreigners. Why should the Federal Reserve Board and the Federal Reserve banks be permitted to finance our competitors in all parts of the world? ("Fed ... Fraud," 2). And why aren't the American people told about such expenditures?

If the media is truly unbiased, independent and completely thorough, why haven't they discussed the Federal Reserve System with the public? Currently, half the states have at least a grassroots movement in action to abolish the Federal Reserve Bank, but there is no press coverage of such movements. Member banks own large percentages of stock in the media companies. To control the media, Federal Reserve bankers call in their loans if the media disagrees with them ("Fed...Fraud," 2).

The Rockefeller Family also controls the Council on Foreign Relations (CFR), whose sole purpose is to aid in stimulating greater interest in foreign affairs and a one-world government. Most major newscasters belong to the Council on Foreign Relations. The CFR controls many major newspapers and magazines as well ("Fed...Fraud," 2).

We American people are as much slaves on a personal level as our government is to the international bankers. We keep right on using the tool they put out here to control us—credit cards. Credit cards imprison us. We no longer are willing to save up to buy something. We have to have it right now. The government has made it easy to have what we want without having to save for it—it is called credit. It seems strange that in a land with so much wealth, only 2 percent of the people own their own homes. At least 60 percent of Americans have at least three credit cards, used to the maximum. Only 1 percent of the people have their cars paid for. We will never be a free people until we rid ourselves of the burden of debt that controls us ("Fed...Fraud," 2).

Monetary System

Dr. Edwin J. Vieira, an attorney at law specializing in Constitutional Law, and the Director of the National Alliance for Constitutional Money, gave an address in Denver, Colorado, to the convention of the National Coalition to Reform Money and Taxes. In that address, he gave a short history of our money system and its problems. He clarified the assumption that monetary reform and tax reform are not at all the same thing. There is no necessary connection between monetary reform and tax reform. There may be all kinds of desirable political or policy connections between the two, but there is no necessary connection between them (Vieira, 1). Consequently, fixing the problems in one area will not fix the problems in the other.

One can have a good taxing system and bad money, and also have good money but a bad taxing system. For example, we could have constitutional money (gold and silver coin) and still have the so-called federal income tax run essentially as a gross receipts tax. The way they implement that tax has absolutely nothing whatsoever to do with the quality of the money they are collecting. The good-tax/bad-tax, good-money/bad-money connection is not a necessary connection (Vieira, 2).

What is the major problem of monetary reform? Ignorance. There are other factors we could add to it, such as apathy and fear, but ignorance is the main one (Vieira, 2).

If you travel around the country and register at hotels, you will find that the persons behind the counter will usually ask, "How do you intend to pay for this?" It would be interesting to answer, "Do you take Federal Reserve Notes?" Invariably, the persons will answer, "No. We take Visa, MasterCard and American Express." Then take out a Federal Reserve Note and show them Where, written across the top, our money says "Federal Reserve Note." The clerk will smile an embarrassed smile. It's kind of funny, and yet it is not funny at all. Most Americans are ignorant of our monetary system to the point that people don't even know what it is they are using as money. They don't even know the name of the thing that they are using to buy things, let alone its source and characteristics or what its problems are (Vieira, 2).

A show on CNN a while back talked about the economic reforms that had to occur in Eastern Europe and the former Soviet Union, and whether the United States should participate in those reforms by providing funds. An economist from the federal government said, "There's an absolute precondition that has to be imposed before any kind of assistance should go over there, and that is, that these countries should agree that there would be an independent central bank to monitor and control their currency" (Vieira, 2). This kind of statement and discussion shows that there is a lot of attention being paid to monetary reforms all over the world.

It's easy to show, and almost impossible to refute, that a dollar is a specific silver coin containing three hundred seventy-one and a quarter grains of fine silver. It has always been that way since the beginning of The World Bankers and the Destruction of America. The Constitution fixes the monetary unit of the United States as this dollar. It empowers Congress to coin silver and gold coins. It very specifically prohibits the government from issuing what the Founding Fathers called "bills of credit" or what we would call today "paper currency" that is redeemable in silver or gold. It is really senseless to talk about adopting a silver- or gold-backed dollar. The fact that so much debate on the Federal Reserve System focuses on this point shows how totally ignorant most of the people are about the subject of American money.

Defining the dollar constitutionally is only the first step in explaining the real nature of the problem we have with the Federal Reserve System.

Problems with the Federal Reserve System

We have to look at three aspects to understand the Federal Reserve System.

The Devolution of Monetary Systems

First, we must keep in mind that the evolution of the Federal Reserve System shows a typical historical devolution or corruption of the monetary systems throughout the world for the last two centuries. This movement is a devolution from commodity money to fiduciary money to fiat money (Vieira, 3). Let's define those three categories of money.

Commodity money is a medium of exchange, a money with intrinsic value in itself, such as a gold or silver coin. In the case of commodity money, the actual commodity, the silver or the gold, is both the medium of exchange and the standard of value (the unit of prices).

The supply of commodity money is self-limited because of the costs of mining, refining and coining the silver and gold. The market will simply not produce more gold and silver coin than is necessary (Vieira 3).

Fiduciary money is a medium of exchange composed of some intrinsically valueless substance (typically paper), which the issuer promises to redeem on demand in commodity money (gold or silver). It is called promissory money because there is a promise to pay in commodity money. An example would be a note backed by gold or silver reserves in a bank. The note is a promise to pay in commodity money, and therefore it represents something of real value.

Private bank notes and government treasury notes are fiduciary monies in general circulation. The paper promise to pay is the medium of day-to-day exchange. The actual money, and the ultimate standard of value, remains the promised medium of payment, which is the silver and gold coins. The supply of fiduciary money is also self-limited by the requirement of redemption. That is, if we have a free market system in which contracts are going to be enforced, fiduciary money will be issued only to the extent that the issuer can satisfy the demands for redemption. We must realize that the "free market" affects this kind of money because the self-limiting aspect of fiduciary money has always failed whenever the government or some powerful private interest group has been able to step in and suspend or repudiate that promise to redeem (Vieira, 3, 4).

Fiat money is backed by nothing. It is composed of some intrinsically valueless substance (usually paper), which the issuer does not promise to redeem either in a commodity or in fiduciary money. The only reason people accept it is because of faith. Because fiat money has no legal connection to commodity money and therefore no real economic cost in terms of production, the supply of fiat money is never self-limiting. The value of fiat money is always largely a matter of public confidence in the economic or political stability of the issuer. Fiat money can be manipulated very easily by anyone involved in its creation.

Historically, every major type of fiat money has self-destructed in what is commonly called "hyperinflation." Hyperinflation is an extreme decrease in purchasing power caused either by unlimited increase in the supply of fiat money by the issuer, or simply by the loss of public confidence in the value of the money, or in the economic or political fortunes of the issuer (Vieira, 4).

The Theory and History of Fiduciary Money

Second, the theory and history of fiduciary money, which is also the theory and history of banking, must focus on the ever-present problem of redemption. Why is it a problem? Because a fiduciary money is a promise to pay a real commodity money. Commodity money in silver or gold coin is itself payment because it contains a fixed weight of precious metal.

But a unit of fiduciary money, a bank note or a treasury note, is only a contingent, an uncertain payment, because it depends on the ability and willingness of the issuer to redeem it. Fiduciary money always threatens to become fraudulent money. The history of fiduciary money has been more or less the history of monetary fraud, both economic and political (Vieira, 4).

The Danger in Issuing Fiduciary Money

Third, the danger of fraud in the issuing of fiduciary money is acute in the case of fractional reserve banking. In fractional reserve banking, the bank is always issuing more units of fiduciary money than it has units of commodity money available for redemption. It counts on the assumption that the majority of its customers will never seek redemption at one time. Modern fractional reserve banking is inherently fraudulent because it is simply impossible for the bank simultaneously to fulfill all its promises to redeem on demand. The bank managers know that complete redemption is impossible. Therefore the promises are false. The bank customers are simply ignorant of how the fractional reserve banking system works (Vieira, 4).

CHAPTER 2:
THE FEDERAL RESERVE SYSTEM

If you want to understand the significance of the Federal Reserve System, you also have to recognize there is no such thing as politically neutral or politically independent money. Ultimately, money is a medium both for storing wealth and for exchanging wealth. Thus, money is a form of property and a mechanism for implementing contracts that transfer property from one person to another.

Even in a free market economy with a limited government, money has a necessarily political character. The degree to which the government protects the money system from private fraud and from public looting reflects the degree to which the government respects and protects private property. A free market economy will necessarily have one kind of money; a mixed economy will have another; a socialist economy another, and so forth. But in every case, the monetary system will accurately reflect the values of the political system. So the debate over whether the Federal Reserve System ought to be politically independent of Congress is completely misdirected (Vieira, 5).

Originally the Constitution made our money independent of all electoral politics by fixing the monetary unit as the dollar, by outlawing bills of credit and by allowing only silver and gold coin to operate as legal tender. Instead of making money politically independent or politically neutral, the Constitution actually settled on one very specific political formula for money—a money of intrinsic value.

The creation of the Federal Reserve System, in 1913, did not make Federal Reserve Notes politically independent or politically neutral. It merely changed the political character of the money system by empowering a small, non-elected clique of self-styled experts and private bankers to control the supply of Federal Reserve Notes, interest rates, and all the other monetary and banking phenomena.

The Federal Reserve System actually politicized money because it enabled politicians, administrators and a few very specially selected special interest groups to exercise the very influence over this country's money and banking systems that the Constitution had originally disallowed. Although control of the monetary and banking systems has serious political significance, the apologists of the Federal Reserve System have been extremely successful in simply removing money and banking issues from the agendas of the political parties, the candidates and anyone else in the political arena (Vieira, 5).

There is no public political discussion about these issues anymore.

1. There is no serious political movement now to propose the immediate restoration of our constitutional money system.
2. No serious political movement demands that all paper currency of private banks be true fiduciary monies.
3. No serious political movement attacks fraudulent fractional reserve banking.

4. No serious political movement denounces the incestuous relationship between the government and the banking industry through the Federal Reserve.

It is vitally important politically that no serious political movement challenges the government's use of the monetary and banking system to regulate the economy. And it is of vital political significance that the general public is simply unable to devise any kind of strategy for dealing with the Federal Reserve System as a supposed agency of the government (Vieira, 5).

The Federal Reserve System, when it testifies before Congress, tells Congress what the policy is going to be, not the other way around. Congress does not control it. Nobody has a handle on this agency (Vieira, 5).

A group that could exercise all these matters, without complaint by any significant part of the public, must be very powerful. The history books do not explain how the apologists for the Federal Reserve were successful in stifling political debate (Vieira, 6). What is clear is that the Federal Reserve was established to remove the Constitution as the controlling agency in national monetary policy and to guarantee that certain special interest groups were disproportionately represented in determining that policy. The result of these things was the setting up of a monopoly.

Levels of the Federal Reserve

Let's look at the Federal Reserve several ways, on several levels.

First Level

We could describe the Federal Reserve System as a tool for stabilizing the inherently fraudulent fractional reserve banking system. The purpose of the Federal Reserve System is not necessarily to do what the bankers want, but it is to do what the bankers need. If you have a regime of commodity money, the bankers employ the inherently fraudulent fractional reserve system. They expand the supply of fiduciary money (bank notes and their demand currencies) beyond the supply of commodity money available.

This action has two effects: 1. It enables bankers to loan more money than they otherwise would, which increases their profits; and 2. It makes the holders of all that fiduciary money unknowing partners with the bankers in those excessive loans. Consequently, it spreads the risk of those loans throughout society (Vieira, 6).

The supply of this inherently fraudulent fiduciary money is limited by the possibility of bankruptcy—lots of people coming forward and asking for redemption. If such a thing happened, the banks would go bankrupt. The bankers then would go out and support legislation designed to insulate the fractional reserve banking system from threats. And they would use propaganda to con the public into believing that the banks were sound. One of the mechanisms for doing that is the so-called deposit insurance scheme. "The government will pay," they claim. "If we fail, the government will pay." Since the government doesn't own the Federal Reserve, it is the people who will pay (Vieira, 6). But of course the people do not know that.

Second Level

Bankers ask the government to authorize what used to be called suspension of specie payments. That means that the bankers simply refuse to fulfill their promises to redeem the fiduciary money with commodity money. This refusal allows the bankers to stay in business, even though they are bankrupt. Suspensions of specie payments are a key indicator of the breakdown of the free-market economy, because they are a governmentally allowed repudiation of contracts (Vieira, 6).

Third Level

To prevent bank runs, the bankers lobby for government permission to repudiate their fiduciary money totally. Instead, they want to convert the fiduciary money into fiat money. There is no problem about bank runs then, because there is nothing that they have to redeem. This action usually requires the government to force the circulation of the fiat currency. They can do so by several methods. For example, the government can:

1. make that money tender in payment of taxes; people will need it to pay their taxes, and that will force circulation;
2. declare that money legal tender for all debts; or
3. outlaw contracts that are payable in any other form of money, especially commodity money.

That is precisely what the government did in that banking crisis in the mid-1930s—it turned Federal Reserve Notes into a fiat legal tender currency, at least in respect to gold coins (Vieira, 6).

These steps would substitute the taxpayers as the ultimate guarantors of the fiat money, instead of the banks and the banks' shareholders. In return for this action, the banks would have to agree to do two things (Vieira, 7):

1. They would have to agree to monetize the public debt—to buy government securities for duly created fiat money, enabling the government to use the fiat money system as an instrument of taxation.
2. They would have to agree to cooperate in some kind of cartel or self-regulatory scheme to control the expansion of the supply of fiat money within limits that maintain public confidence. In other words, the government and the banks would agree to divide the

amount that can be looted from the general public by manipulation of the money supply. They would agree to this so that the system would not collapse and the public would not see that they are the ones paying the bills.

Fractional Reserve Banking System

Those agreements explain the fractional reserve banking system. It is a conspiracy between the public officials and the bankers to take money from the American people. The Federal Reserve is simply a very elaborate and complicated device that has been set up to accomplish these simple ends in a highly deceptive way. The Federal Reserve System was begun as the response of bankers and their political cronies to failures in the fractional reserve banking system at the local or regional levels. They created a national-level system to regulate it all (Vieira, 7).

Actually, real fiat money came into existence in this country only in 1968. We had repudiation of the promise to pay gold in 1933. We had a repudiation of the promise to redeem all currency, or any currency, in silver in 1967 and 1968. It wasn't until June 1968 that we had, for the first time in this country, a true fiat currency in the Federal Reserve Note. Since then we have seen a geometrically accelerating breakdown in the monetary and banking systems (Vieira, 7).

Today, we suffer under a regime of fiat currency and unlimited fractional reserve banking. The Federal Reserve plays a simple but vital role. The public confidence in the monetary banking system weakens because of the effect of over-expansion of the supply of fiat money. Fiat money follows the same path—expansion, expansion and expansion. The Federal Reserve jumps in to "restore confidence" by what they call "fighting inflation." But the Federal Reserve will never fight inflation so drastically that it precipitates a genuine economic collapse or seriously endangers the long-term interests of the banking cartel, its satellite industries or its political cronies (Vieira, 7).

There is a problem. Any system of fractional reserve banking suffers from an inherent instability that increases over time because fractional reserve banking is a kind of pyramid scheme (Vieira, 7). Consequently, we can expect that the remaining lifetime of the Federal Reserve confidence game will be relatively short (Vieira, 8).

The Federal Reserve System is not simply a control mechanism for the national banking cartel. It is one of the most important mechanisms in a pervasive system of economic regulations that has been set up in this country. This explains the political independence of the Federal Reserve System. If an administrative state is to regulate the economy with relative autonomy from the electoral public and most special interest groups, then the monetary agency has to claim political independence (Vieira, 8).

The political independence of the Federal Reserve is precisely what one would expect it to claim when it is a part of an anti-democratic mechanism of economic and political control. The fact that no constitutional branch of the national government—not the Congress, not the President, not the Judiciary—ever disputes the Federal Reserve System's supposed independence shows the truth of the claim.

Contemporary political money, and the banking system that generates it, have five major consequences (Vieira, 8).

    1. Political money is the prime means by which the government operates a system of hidden taxation through increases in the supply of money, the inflation mechanism. Inflation of the money supply

is a hidden form of taxation. One of the ways in which the government can redistribute real wealth from citizens to the state is by changing the amount of money in circulation. That's a hidden tax (Vieira, 1).

2. By operating a system of hidden taxation, modern political money enables the ruling elite of the country to redistribute the nation's wealth from one group to another. The American Institute for Economic Research, Great Barrington, Massachusetts, puts out a paper every year describing how much money has been redistributed by inflation since World War II. The last one showed that over six trillion dollars had been redistributed through inflation. A fantastic loss of wealth in the United States has occurred—a minimum six trillion dollar loss of wealth since World War II because of the Federal Reserve System.

3. By functioning as a mechanism for redistributing wealth, modern political money systematically corrupts the electoral process because it enables politicians to buy votes with promises of new government spending programs made possible only by the banking system's ability to monetize the public debt (Vieira, 8).

4. By tying the banks to the public debt, modern political money licenses the banks to loot the public treasury. First, by guaranteeing Federal Reserve Notes as obligations of the United States, calling them legal tender. And second, by providing bailouts to the bankers through the FSLIC, the RTC, the FDIC or whatever, when the scheme of inherently fraudulent fractional reserve banking collapses. We can see that happening. Hundreds of millions for the recent Savings and Loan bailout.

How much for the coming commercial bank bailout? How much is the bailout of the insurance companies going to cost? How much for pension funds? (Vieira, 9).

5. Modern political money and political banking function as a key mechanism in the scheme of economic planning that misdirects and wastes resources, and thereby lowers the standard of living of most Americans. Communism is collapsing throughout Eastern Europe and the Soviet Union, but we have still got it here (Vieira, 9).

What We Can Do About It

A reform of the Federal Reserve by institutional changes, or by the possibility of going to some supranational banking cartel or world banking system, a New World Order banking system, is ahead.

The steps for change can be documented historically, based on early instances of American constitutional and statutory law. We must follow these steps to bring the United States' monetary and banking systems back into conformance with constitutional law (Vieira, 9).

First, we have to declare unconstitutional:

1. the Federal Reserve Act of 1913,
2. the seizure of gold coin in 1933, and
3. the outlawing in 1934 of private contracts calling for payment in gold or silver.

We have to condemn the basic unconstitutional steps that were taken by the government to establish ultimately this fiat currency system.

Second, we have to disestablish the Federal Reserve System and privatize the few politically legitimate and economically useful functions that it has that would be legitimate and useful for private banks —as a national clearing house for example.

Third, we would definitely have to terminate the status of Federal Reserve Notes as obligations of the United States and as legal tender for all debts. There is no constitutional justification for the American taxpayer to be the ultimate guarantor for the investment schemes of banks, savings & loans, and the Federal Reserve System.

Fourth, we have to dedicate to the restoration of the constitutional money system the gold that was unconstitutionally seized from the American people in 1933 (now held by the United States Treasury) (Vieira, 9).

Most of the gold held in Fort Knox and at West Point is what is called "coin melt" gold. It is the 90 percent pure gold that was melted down from ingots, from coins seized during the 1933 seizure. The government was engaged in receiving stolen goods at that time—all of that money has to be returned to those from whom it was taken. It is to be used for the purpose of restoring the monetary system (Vieira, 10).

We must re-value, in terms of constitutional dollars, all other outstanding contracts that are now payable in Federal Reserve Notes. The contracts must have some real value attached to them. The real value would be their value in constitutional dollars (Vieira, 10).

We must begin the free coinage of gold and silver coin, not the limited coinage done now (the American Eagle coins for example), but coining as much gold and silver as people want to bring into the mints.

We have to adopt all the foreign silver and gold coins as money of the United States—what Congress did by monetizing all the gold and silver of the world, instantly.

Those people who talk about there not being enough gold or silver in circulation don't know what they are talking about. It's not in circulation because it is not treated as money. When we start saying that it is money, it will start coming out from the coffers all over. And we must regulate the value of all those coins, and pro-hibit the practice of fraudulent fractional reserve banking schemes (Vieira, 10).

This is not a visionary program. It will be very difficult politically to put into effect, but it is not visionary because these things have happened twice before. They happened once at the end of the war of Independence, when we had the same kind of rotting vegetable currency (continental currency)—the same bills of credit. There was no gold and silver coin in circulation. The economy was prostrate. They took all of these steps, and there was an economic recovery (Vieira, 10).

Second, it happened in the South following the Civil War. The Confederate currency was destroyed. The country was in economic trouble and was under the military occupation when these steps were taken. They were taken in the North as well—the entire country (Vieira, 10). The currency was turned back to redeemable or fiduciary paper currency (Vieira, 11).

It can be done again. The only question is whether the American people want it to be done and have the gumption to make the politicians do it (Vieira, 11).

CHAPTER 3:
CONGRESS AND OUR MONEY

In an interview on "Income Taxes and Government Fraud" with Susan B. Anthony, John E. Trumane stated, "In 1933 we know now that the federal government was bankrupted, and whatever gold was in the U.S. Treasury was handed over to the Federal Reserve Corporation, which is not a federal government agency. Roosevelt declared a national emergency and closed the banks for three days" (Trumane, 1).

Congress can extract only so much money out of the economy. If private owners become bankrupt, then the banks that are behind this syndicate become the owners of all assets in this country. By encouraging Congress to spend money it doesn't have, the government forces Congress to turn around and put "liens" on American labor and American private property for collateral (Trumane, 1).

Brussels, Belgium, is the center of the hub of the banking syndicate, and that hub is of course loaning huge sums to various governments around the world, including the Congress of the United States (Anthony, 1). It's like this: The more collateral I have, the more money I can borrow from banks and the more I can secure. Governments are securing their international debt by putting liens on the persons and property of their citizens (Trumane, 2).

Think of it very simply as walking into a department

store and saying to the salesman, "I really like that refrigerator over there. I want to buy it. Ship it to my home tomorrow, and send the bill to Willy Brown." The next day when Willy Brown opens his mail, he'll say, "What's this? I didn't buy this refrigerator." This is kind of like what is happening in our monetary system. The department store is the Federal Reserve. They are supplying Federal Reserve Notes. Willy Brown is the American people, and the one who bought the refrigerator represents Congress. And Congress is saying, "Don't send the bill to me, send it to the American people. And you can put a lien on their property to force them to pay." That's the fraud (Trumane, 2).

The fraud is that Congress bankrupted the U.S. Treasury and turned all its gold over to the Federal Reserve banks (which are not federal agencies). The Federal Reserve is a "municipal corporation" created by an act of Congress, but it is still a corporation. And all that gold is now in its hands (Trumane, 2).

A Manipulated Economy

The Federal Reserve manipulates the economy to cause inflation by controlling the money supply and interest rates. Inflation puts tremendous pressure on the middle class to turn over their assets, in order to finance their essentials of food, shelter and clothing. It is no wonder that land has become so expensive. And it is no wonder that labor has become so expensive, transferring a great deal of wealth out of the hands of the middle class and the millions of people who work so hard, day after day, and into the hands of the ruling elite. It is systematically designed to do that; it is not happening by coincidence (Trumane, 2).

The report of the Peter Grace Commission documented in writing, with proof, that the individual income tax revenues that the IRS collects and extracts are not going to pay for any government services. They are going to pay for interest on the national debt. And they are going to pay for transfer payments to the people who are on the receiving end of Social Security. Money is being taken out of the economy and transferred elsewhere, either into Social Security beneficiaries or into the private stockholders of the Federal Reserve system (Trumane, 2).

How much interest are the American people paying on five to six trillion dollars, which the national debt is approaching? They admit that it is approaching six trillion dollars. It is probably more like 18 trillion. They are paying 400 billion dollars annually to discharge interest alone on the national debt they have accrued. That doesn't do anything to reduce the principal. And the government continues to enlarge that principal every year (Trumane, 2).

Congress was responsible for passing the Federal Reserve Act in the first place. And their allowing it to remain on the books will bankrupt all the private assets throughout the country (Trumane, 2).

What We Can Do

When Anthony asked Trumane what the ordinary citizen who is fed up with his money being squandered can do, Trumane answered this way:

First, we have to take steps to eliminate our ignorance because the Law is in place. The Law is there to defend our rights. The purpose of the Constitution is, above all, to protect individual rights. If the American people want to fight this thing, they can do so by first understanding the Law and then pointing out to people in government that they are violating the Law, by forcefully extracting what is a voluntary system of taxation. Congress is chained by the Constitution to use Thomas Jefferson's terminology. They cannot go out and forcibly extract our voluntary participation in their third-party debt scheme and do so lawfully (Trumane, 3).

Is the government now in economic distress? Yes and no. The Congress can always turn to the Federal Reserve System to bail out their deficit. If their deficit happens to skyrocket this year because people haven't sent their taxes in, Congress can always turn to the Federal Reserve, as they have been doing all along, to borrow more money into circulation. And then they will turn around and try to extract that much more in interest payments from the American people. It doesn't put government in economic distress, but it puts the people in economic distress. This system has a built-in safety valve. Congress can turn around and borrow more Federal Reserve Notes by creating bonds (Trumane, 3).

Congress takes in X amount in revenues from individual income taxes and excise taxes and corporate taxes. But there is always a shortfall. Because they want to spend 300 or 400 billion each year, and this is more than they take in, what do they do? They get printing presses. They put ink on paper and they call them bonds. And they float those bonds on the market. Hopefully, people with money will buy them up. Some Americans have enough money to buy bonds issued by the Treasury. Those who do sit on a piece of paper that is supposed to pay so much interest.

But the problem is that there isn't enough slack money in the economy for all private, wage-earning, hardworking Americans to buy up all these bonds every year. So Congress always ends up with a huge number of unsold bonds. What do they do? They march across the street to the Federal Reserve, and say, "Federal Reserve, will you buy these bonds from us?" And the Federal Reserve agrees to do so, but the Federal Reserve also stipulates the amount of interest the Government will pay. Congress has to take the deal because there is nobody else on the planet with that kind of money. The Federal Reserve is sitting on the largest concentration of wealth that has ever been accumulated in the world. So it doesn't mind billing Congress again every year. The Federal Reserve is doing this to every country on the planet (Trumane, 3, 4).

Congress has to take the deal because it has to balance its budget. So the bonds go into the vaults of the Federal Reserve. The Bureau of Printing and Engraving then prints out the equivalent number of Federal Reserve Notes. The Federal Reserve notes are the property of the Federal Reserve System; they are not the property of the U.S. Treasury. But Congress injects these Notes into the economy by using them to pay Congressmen and Senators and judges and military officers and GIs and janitors—all the government's employees. Now the money is put into the economy (Anthony 4).

CHAPTER 4:
INFLATION AND INTEREST

If the Federal Reserve puts money into the economy like that, if the money supply grows faster than the aggregate sum of the goods and services exchanged in the economy, then we have inflation. Higher prices are not the cause of inflation; higher prices are the effect of inflation. Inflation is defined as a disproportionate increase in the money supply relative to the quantity of goods and services being exchanged. That means that there is more money out there. People will pay higher prices so they can outbid other buyers, and prices will rise (Anthony, 4).

How, then, do we prevent inflation as the government continues to inject money into the economy? We must do something that will pull money out of the economy. That is where the IRS comes in. They are a collection agency (sometimes compared to a vacuum). The Federal Reserve pumps cash and credit into the economy. The IRS sucks it out of the economy. And the controllers are very skillfully shifting the rates of these two actions to set waves of recession and inflation pouring through the economy. The aggregate level rises up and down, and the controllers sit back with all this money to spend and play this big game (Trumane, 4).

Susan B. Anthony asked Trumane whether the Japanese and Iraqis had their hands in the pot. Trumane answered that we have an international economy, and a lot of those bonds are spread around the country and around the world. So the bond holders are not just the American middle class, not just the Federal Reserve, but a lot of foreign countries as well (Trumane, 4). More and more ties are being formed with financial institutions around the world. Such ties lead to an opening for a World Bank. Our new would-be rulers (Global Banking) are trying to change our whole racial, social, religious and political order, but they will not change the debt-money-economic systems, which they use to rule us. The Book of Proverbs warns us "the borrower is servant to the lender" (Prov. 22:7).

Since the U.S. Congress has not issued Constitutional money since 1863, the people are forced to borrow the "created credit" of the monopoly bankers and to pay them high rates of interest in order to have money to carry on trade and commerce. That's one form of income and wealth for bankers.

The bankers also have another method of drawing large amounts of wealth. The banks that control the money at the top are able to approve or disapprove large loans to large and successful corporations. Refusal of a loan may bring about a reduction in the selling price of the corporation's stock.

After the price is depressed, the bankers' agents will then buy large blocks of the company's stock. Then, if the bank later decides to approve a multimillion dollar loan to the company, the stock prices rise and the shares are sold for a profit. Today the actual buys and sells are not necessary, for the Federal Reserve Board need only announce to the newspapers an increase or decrease in its "discount rate" to send stocks soaring or crashing.

The bankers and their agents have purchased secret or open control of many large corporations in America. They then force the corporations to borrow huge sums from their banks so that corporate earnings are siphoned off in the form of interest to the banks. Thus banks can make a profit even when stock prices are depressed.

Under this system where new debt always exceeds new money, no matter how much or how little is borrowed, the total debt increasingly outstrips the amount of money available to pay the debt. The people can never get out of debt.

The Tyranny of Compound Interest

When a person goes to a banker to borrow $100,000 to purchase a home or property, the bank clerk has the borrower agree to pay back the loan plus interest. If the interest is 8.25 percent, for 30 years (that is high for these days, but it is an unsecured loan and will show as an example), the borrower must agree to pay $751.27 per month for a total of $270,456.00.

The bank clerk then requires the person to assign to the banker the right of ownership of the property if the borrower does not make the payments. The bank clerk gives the borrower a check for $100,000 (or a $100,000 deposit slip, crediting the borrower's account with the money).

The borrower then writes checks to the builders, workers or escrow people, who in turn write checks to pay their own company bills. So $100,000 of new "checkbook" money is added to the "money in circulation." However, the flaw now shows up. The only new money created and put into circulation is the amount of the loan—the $100,000. The money to pay the interest is NOT created, and therefore was NOT added to the "money in circulation."

Even so, this borrower must earn and take out of circulation $270,456.00 or $170,456.00 more than he put in circulation when he borrowed the original money.

Every new loan puts the same process in operation. Each borrower adds a small sum to the total money supply when he borrows, but the payment on the loan then deducts a much larger sum from the total money supply. Since this has happened millions of times over the past few years, you can see why the United States has gone from being a prosperous, debt-free nation to a debt-ridden nation where practically every home, farm and business is paying interest to the bankers. There is therefore no way all debtors can pay off the money lenders.

In the millions of transactions made each year, like that just discussed, very little actual currency will change hands. About 95 percent of all "cash" transactions in the US are transactions by check. Realize that banks must hold only 10 percent of their deposits on site in cash at any given time. This means that 90 percent of all deposits, though they are actually held by the bank, are not present in the form of actual cash currency. Consequently, the banker is relatively safe to "create" that so-called loan by writing the check or deposit slip not against actual money, but against your promise to pay it back. The cost to the banker is paper, ink and a few dollars of overhead for each transaction.

National Economics

The same principles apply to national economies as well as to individual economies. For example, when a nation gets in trouble, along comes the International Monetary Fund and the World Bank to loan more money so that the nation in question can keep up with the interest repayments. The different national economies are like ships in the sea. All these ships are sinking, but some are going down faster than others. Many nations are not greedy, and in fact want to help other countries in trouble. While some ships are sinking, we also see sinking ships that are trying to bail out other sinking ships so as to prolong the inevitable (Fraser and Beeston, 11).

No private banks would exist to rob the people if we

followed the original Constitutional system. Government banks under the control of the people's representatives would issue and control all money and credit. They would issue actual currency as well as limited credit at no interest for the purchase of capital goods, such as homes. A $100,000 loan would require only $100,000 repayment. All workers on the home would get paid just as they do now, but the banks would not collect an additional $170,456.00 in interest.

Under the present system, the extra burden of interest forces workers and businesses to demand more money for the work and goods to pay their own ever increasing debts and taxes. This increase in prices and wages is inflation. Bankers, politicians and economists blame it on everything but the real cause—the interest levied on money and debt by bankers. Inflation benefits the moneylenders since it wipes out the savings of one generation so they are not able to finance or help the next generation. The next generation, then, must again borrow from the moneylenders and pay large amounts of interest.

The elimination of the interest payments and debt would be the equivalent of a 50 percent raise in the purchasing power of every worker. This would mean about $400 billion yearly in property and wealth that currently goes to banks.

The Daily Eagle reported that the power of banks is stupendous, both in granting loans and in recalling them arbitrarily. Court decisions may be the beginning of the end of some of their powers. For example, note the following decisions:

- A Minnesota Trial Court decided to hold the Federal Reserve Act unconstitutional and void,
- The National Banking Act was declared unconstitutional and void,
- A mortgage acquired by the First National Bank of Montgomery, Minnesota, along with a foreclosure

and the Sheriff's sale was declared void (*Daily Eagle*, 1).

These decisions have the effect of declaring all private mortgages on real and personal property, and all US and state bonds held by the Federal Reserve, national and state banks, to be null and void. Upon such decisions hangs the question of freedom or slavery to the world's banking systems. Decisions such as these are only a beginning, and many people hoped for much more. Unfortunately, time has gone by and these decisions did not accomplish the breakthrough expected. The system of international banking and the elite still rules.

In fact, the *Business Week* of December 6, 2004, did a special report on the effects of globalization on trades, business, Gross National Product and labor in general. The report stated, "Trade economists are struggling to reconcile traditional theories with emerging global realities" (117). In the section of the report titled "End of the Big Bank Bonanza," we learn that "Banks are facing hurdles in their quest to boost earnings... [because] the hot credit-card and mortgage-refi business are cooling as interest rates rise [and] regulatory costs are rising because of new laws" (126). The more major media sources discuss globalization, the more easily Americans will come to accept it as inevitable. As the American people get further into debt, the more necessary the global bank will seem.

These steps towards a Global Bank are simple. Notice the progression of acceptance.

- The World Bank—This lends money to finance projects in the Third World to meet the needs of the multinationals.
- The International Monetary Fund (IMF)—When poor countries get into Elite-engineered financial

trouble, the IMF intervenes to offer more loans (thereby increasing the debt) on the condition that the Elite's policies are followed. Those policies would include giving up land to grow crops in order to produce luxury crops for exportation.
- The European Monetary Union (EU)—The move by the European Union towards a centralized bank and single currency will follow. Actually this step has already begun with the UK's opt-out clause in the Maastricht Treaty being overruled by another.
- Control of Food—Natural agricultural seeds will be replaced with patented, genetically engineered ones. According to UN estimates, 75 percent of genetic diversity in agricultural crops has been lost this century and in England. The situation now is that Third World countries must pay royalties to the multinational companies for genetically engineered seeds (Fraser and Beeston, 9).

Truth, Not Ignorance
The United States will not shake off her banker-controlled dictatorship as long as the people are ignorant of the hidden controllers. Banking concerns, which control most of the governments of the nations, and most sources of information, are afraid of only one thing—an awakened patriotic citizenry, armed with the truth. How do we find out the truth? The media will not help inform the people. The media are working for the banker-owned United States, in a banker-owned world under a banker-owned world government. This is the main point of all the talk of a New World Order.

Fraser and Beeston recommend that in order to regain control over our financial system we learn about the economic treaties that fall under the Global Agreement on Trade and Tariffs (GATT), such as the North American Free Trade Agreement (NAFTA), Asia Pacific

THE WORLD BANKERS AND THE DESTRUCTION OF AMERICA

Economic Cooperation (APEC), and the European Union (EU). These have been designed to lower the standard of living in the developed nations via a transfer of wealth. With these treaties, governments remove tariffs and trade protections, thus forcing small business to compete on equal terms with transnational corporations. They call it "economic rationalism." Economic rationalism is based on a free market working in a laissez-faire (free enterprise) society. It won't work otherwise (Fraser and Beeston, 11).

Edward Griffin, in a speech titled "How the Federal Reserve Act Was Made into Law," reveals how the Federal Reserve was created, as well as the background of the International Monetary Fund/World Bank. Even more informative is Griffin's book, *The Creature from Jekyll Island: A Second Look at the Federal Reserve*. In the book, he states that since the System makes it profitable for banks to make large, unsound loans, then the banks will make that kind of loan. Banks love those loans, for they can collect interest—hence they don't care if the principal is ever paid. In fact, banks prefer that the principal is never paid, because they know they cannot lose. The Federal Reserve guarantees that massive loans that go into default will not be allowed to seriously affect the issuing bank. So the banks cannot lose.

For credit card "loans," bank mortgages and most car loans, the banks do not actually "loan" anything—not one penny of actual money. Instead, the banks use the papers people sign (their promise to pay the bank) to "create" the money in order to fund the loans (Griffin, 2).

Griffin also points out that the fears of our Founding Fathers were appropriate and realistic. The Federal Reserve is the fourth central bank the United States has had. The previous three crashed in inevitable inflation and economic disaster (Griffin, 1).

Griffin offers a realistic plan for saving our country and

ourselves. The full plan is explained in his book *The Creature from Jekyll Island*. Griffin outlines a procedure by which the Federal Reserve can be abolished, the national debt paid and the country returned to a sound monetary system based on silver and gold (Griffin, 2). Griffin sees a possible doomsday, as a severe financial crash would cause panicked Americans to accept a World Bank to "rescue" them with a world currency. The IMF/World Bank is already functioning—in conjunction with the Federal Reserve—as a world central bank. A world currency is already designed, waiting for a crisis to justify its introduction. In the past decade, seemingly insane spending both at home and abroad has deliberately weakened the US. As just one example, remember President Clinton's quick promise to send billions of dollars to Poland, Ukraine, and the Baltic countries (Griffin, 1).

CHAPTER 5: CONCLUSION

Will world banking have a chance to come to the free United States of America? Most people would automatically say "no." However, so many people are in debt so deeply that they will never see their way out on their own. Therefore, they are especially vulnerable to a world banking and money system. Subtle moves toward the New World Order have been furthered by current banking and economic systems. Remember that those who own the money control the world.

There will always be vastly more money in circulation than there is actual wealth to back it up. And when the borrowers run out of money to pay their lenders, they have two choices: to become enslaved to their debtors or to conquer them. Through these facts of daily life, we see the possibility of an economic takeover of our country.

BIBLIOGRAPHY
AND FURTHER READING

"A Landmark Decision." 1969. *The Daily Eagle*, Issue of Feb. 7.

Allen, Gary. 1971. *None Dare Call It Conspiracy*. Seal Beach, CA: Concord Press.

Anthony, Susan B. Interview with John E. Trumane, "Income Taxes and Government Fraud." See the following website:
http://www9.pair.com/xpoez/money/fraud.html.

"The China Price." 2004. Special Report. *Business Week*, December 6, p. 102ff.

Cook, Peter, M.Sc., C.M.E., Comp. & Editor. 1993. *What Banks Don't Want You to Know*. Monetary Science Publishing.

Fraser, Ivan, and Mark Beeston. "The Brotherhood and the Manipulation of Society." See the following:
http://www.mysteriesmegasite.com/main/bigsearch /newworldorder.html.

"Global Diffusion of Plant Biotechnology." 2004. *Business Week*, December 20, p. 75.

Griffin, G. Edward. 1993. "Understanding the Game," *The Creature from Jekyll Island*. Review by Jane Ingrahm, "Killing the Banking Beast." Audio.

Holzer, Henry Mark. 1981. *How Americans Lost Their Right to Own God and Became Criminals in the Process*. Committee for Monetary Research and Education, Inc., Monograph #35.

"The Federal Reserve Fraud,"
http://www.biblebelievers.org.au/moneymad.htm

Trumane, John E. Interview with Susan B. Anthony. "Income Taxes and Government Fraud."
http://www9.pair.com/xpoez/money/fraud.html.

Vieira, Edwin J., Jr. 1991. *Return to Constitutional Money*. Independent Hill, Virginia: National Alliance for Constitutional Money, August 30.

ONE FINAL WORD

America as we know her will cease to exist unless Americans stop the current trends.

America is in peril. Various forces seek to destroy what her Founding Fathers established by the grace of God.

The United States of America was founded as a Christian nation, for that is what the vast majority of Americans were. I believe the majority of Americans still are Christians. A nation is what its people are.

America was intended to be a Holy Land, divinely set apart by God as a light shining on a hill. Right now, America is in shackles and her freedom is in jeopardy. A people may never secure its freedom once and for all time; it must be ready to forever pay the price to preserve its freedom until the Almighty restores the lost paradise.

Americans obviously have tough decisions to make.

PROPHETIC WARNINGS
TO AMERICA

"If men, through fear, fraud, or mistake, should in terms renounce or give up any natural right, the eternal law of reason and the grand end of society would absolutely vacate such renunciation. The right to freedom being the gift of god, it is not in the power of man to alienate this gift and voluntarily become a slave."

—Samuel Adams
The Father of the American Revolution

"We do not have a government armed with suffered power to tame the animal passions of mankind. The Constitution is made only for a moral and a religious people. It is wholly inadequate for the government of any other."

—President John Adams

"If ever time should come, when vain and aspiring men shall possess the highest seats in Government, our country will stand in need of its experienced patriots to prevent its ruin."

—Samuel Adams

"Among the natural rights of the Colonists are these: First, a right to life; Secondly, to liberty; Thirdly, to property; together with the right to support and defend them in the best manner they can."

—Samuel Adams
"Rights of the Colonists," November 1772

"You need only reflect that one of the best ways to get yourself a reputation as a dangerous citizen these days is to go about repeating the very phrases which our founding fathers used in their struggle for independence."

—*C. A. Beard*

"When they came to Capernaum those who collected tax money came to Peter and said, 'Does your master not pay taxes?' He said, 'Yes.' When he came into the house Jesus stopped him, saying, 'What do you think, Simon? From whom do the kings of the earth take custom or taxes? From their own children, or from strangers?' Peter replied, 'From strangers.' Jesus said, 'Then the children are free' " (*Mt. 17:24–26*).

—*The Holy Bible*

"Property: Rightful dominion over external objects; ownership; the unrestricted and exclusive right to a thing; Property is the highest right a man can have to anything."

—*Black's Law Dictionary, Second Edition, 1891*

"Income Tax: A tax on the yearly profits arising from property, professions, trades, and offices."

—*Black's Law Dictionary Second Edition, 1891*

"Our task of creating a Socialist America can only succeed when those who would resist us have been totally disarmed."

—*Sarah Brady*

"I do solemnly swear that I will support and defend the Constitution of the United States against all enemies, foreign and domestic; that I will bear true faith and allegiance to the same; that I take this obligation freely, without any mental reservation or purpose of evasion: and that I will well and faithfully discharge the duties of the office on which I am about to enter. So help me, God."

—Congressional Oath of Office

"As civil rulers, not having their duty to the people duly before them, may attempt to tyrannize, and as the military forces which must be occasionally raised to defend our country, might pervert their power to the injury of their fellow citizens, the people are confirmed by the next article [the Second Amendment] in their right to keep and bear their private arms."

—Trence Coxe under the pseudonym "A Pennsylvanian" From "Remarks on the First Part of the Amendments to the Federal Constitution," Published in the Philadelphia Federal Gazette, 18 June 1789

"Find out just what the people will submit to, and you have found out the exact amount of injustice and wrong which will be imposed upon them; and these will continue until they are resisted with either words or blows, or with both. The limits of tyrants are prescribed by the endurance of those whom they oppress."

—Frederick Douglas (1857)

"The hardest thing in the world to understand is the income tax."

—Albert Einstein

"It is well that the people of the nation do not understand our banking and monetary system, for if they did, I believe there would be a revolution before tomorrow morning"

—Henry Ford

"Those who give up essential liberties for temporary safety deserve neither liberty nor safety."

—Benjamin Franklin

"Step by Step the International Financiers and those who represent them gain ownership of real assets as collateral for the debt interest. Now these assets are not directly acquired by the Federal Reserve but the wealth is acquired through the continual process of inflation which is merely the result of the flooding of the economy with fiat money. This system ensures that the wealth is slowly transferred from the middle class to the upper class."

—Fraser and Beeston

"What, sir, is the use of a militia? It is to prevent the establishment of a standing army, the bane of liberty... Whenever Governments mean to invade the rights and liberties of the people, they always attempt to destroy the militia, in order to raise an army upon their ruins."

—Representative Elbridge Gerry, Massachusetts, I Annals of Congress at 750, 8/17/1789

"The legal right of the taxpayer to decrease the amount of what otherwise would be his taxes or altogether avoid them by means which the law permits, cannot be doubted."

—Gregory v. Helvering, 293 U.S. 465

"The great object is that everyman be armed. Everyone who is able may have a gun."

—Patrick Henry At the Virginia Convention on the ratification of the Constitution

"I know not what course others may take, but as for me, give me liberty or give me death."
—*Patrick Henry*

"The best yardstick of the effectiveness of the fight against Communism is the fury of the smear attacks against the fighter."
—*J. Edgar Hoover*

"The democracy will cease to exist when you take away from those who are willing to work and give to those who would not."
—*President Thomas Jefferson*

"To compel a man to subsidize with his taxes the propagation of ideas which he disbelieves and abhors is sinful and tyrannical."
—*President Thomas Jefferson*

"When we get piled upon one another in large cities, as in Europe, we shall become as corrupt as Europe."

—*President Thomas Jefferson*
"Still one thing more, fellow citizens, a wise and frugal government which shall restrain men from injuring one another, shall leave them otherwise free to regulate their own pursuits of industry and improvement, and shall not take from the mouth of labor the bread it has earned. This is the sum of good government."
—*President Thomas Jefferson, First Inaugural Address*

"I predict future happiness for Americans if they can prevent the government from wasting the labors of the people under the pretense of taking care of them."
—*President Thomas Jefferson*

"Fear can only prevail when victims are ignorant of the facts."
—*President Thomas Jefferson*

"The strongest reason for the people to retain the right to keep and bear arms is, as a last resort, to protect themselves against tyranny in government."
—*President Thomas Jefferson*

"No free man shall ever be debarred the use of arms."
—*President Thomas Jefferson*

"Peace, commerce, and honest friendship with all nations, entangling alliances with none."
—*President Thomas Jefferson, First Inaugural Address*

"A government that is large enough to supply everything you need is large enough to take everything you have."
—*President Thomas Jefferson*

"I sincerely believe that banking institutions are more dangerous to our liberties than standing armies. If the American people ever allow private banks to control the issue of their currency, first by inflation, then by deflation, the banks and corporations that will grow up around the banks will deprive the people of all property until their children wake up homeless on the continent their fathers conquered."
—*President Thomas Jefferson*

"The tree of liberty must be watered periodically with the blood of tyrants and patriots alike. It is its natural manure."
—*President Thomas Jefferson*

"A strong body makes the mind strong. As to the species of exercises, I advise the gun. While this gives moderate exercise to the body, it gives boldness, enterprise and independence to the mind. Games played with the ball and others of that nature, are too violent for the body and stamp no character on the mind. Let your gun therefore be the constant companion of your walks."
—President Thomas Jefferson

"The high office of President has been used to foment a plot to destroy the American's freedom, and before I leave office I must inform the citizen of his plight."
—President John F. Kennedy
At Columbia University, ten days before his assassination

"We shall cause the United States to spend itself to destruction."
—Lenin

"This nation can never be conquered from without. If it is ever to fall it will be from within."
—President Abraham Lincoln

"As usurpation is the exercise of power, which another hath a right to; so tyranny is the exercise of power beyond right, which nobody can have a right to."
—John Locke, "Of Civil Government," 1689

"I believe there are more instances of the abridgment of freedom of the people by gradual and silent encroachment of those in power than by violent and sudden usurpations."
—President James Madison

"The Federal Reserve Bank is 'a super-state' controlled by international bankers and international industrialists acting together to enslave the world for their own pleasure."

—Former Congressman Louis McFadden
Former Chairman, House Committee on Banking and
Currency

"We have in this country one of the most corrupt institutions the world has ever known. I refer to the Federal Reserve Board and the Federal Reserve Banks...They are, not government institutions. They are private monopolies which prey upon the people of these United States for the benefit of themselves and their foreign customers..."

—Senator Louis T. McFadden
Chairman of the U.S. Banking & Currency Commission

"Those that create and issue the money and credit direct the policies of government and hold in their hands the destiny of the people."

—Reginald McKenna
Former President of the Midlands Bank of England

"In the United States today we have in effect two governments. We have the duly constituted government. Then we have an independent, uncontrolled and uncoordinated government in the Federal Reserve System, operating the money powers reserved to Congress by the Constitution"

—Congressman Wright Patman
Former Chairman of the House Banking Committee

"Patriotism means to stand by the country. It does not mean to stand by the President or any other public office save exactly to the degree in which he himself stands by the country."

—President Theodore Roosevelt

"No one is bound to obey an unconstitutional law and no courts are bound to enforce it."

—Sixteenth American Jurisprudence
Second Edition, Section 177

"The highest level of prosperity occurs when there is a free-market economy and a minimum of government regulations."

—Adam Smith, "The Wealth of Nations"

"'Income,' as used in the statute should be given the meaning so as not to include everything that comes in. The true function of the words 'gain' and 'profit' is to limit the meaning of the word income."

—So. Pacific v. Lower, 238 F 847

"All socialism involves slavery."

—Herbert Spencer

"All government without the consent of the governed is the very definition of slavery."

—Jonathan Swift

"The tax power has been used by the national government as a weapon to take over, one by one, subjects traditionally within the orbit of state police power."

—Chief Justice Taft

"All laws which are repugnant to the Constitution are null and void."

—U.S. Supreme Court
Marbury v. Madison, 2Cranch 5 U.S. (1803)

"None are more hopelessly enslaved than those who falsely believe they are free."

—Johann W. Von Goethe

"It is impossible to rightly govern the world without God or the Bible." And "Reason and experience forbid us to expect public morality in the absence of religious principle."

—*President George Washington*

"Government is not reason; it is not eloquence; it is force! Like fire, it is a dangerous servant and a fearful master."

—*President George Washington*

"God grants liberty only to those who love it, and are always ready to guard and defend it."

—*Daniel Webster*

"An Unconstitutional Act is not a law; it confers no rights; it imposes no duties; it affords no protection; it creates no office; it is, in legal contemplation, as inoperative as though it had never been passed."

—*U.S. Supreme Court Norton V. Shelby County, 118 U.S. 425, 442*

"If we abide by the principles taught in the Bible, our nation will go on prospering."

—*Daniel Webster*

"God grants liberty only to those who love it, and are always ready to guard and defend it."

—*Daniel Webster*

"One of the main purposes for the control and power of the Establishment media is to keep the masses deceived and ignorant about their rights and oppressions of their rights."

—*Charles Weisman*

COMMUNIST RULES FOR REVOLUTION

Captured by the Allies in Dusseldorf, Germany
1919

A. Corrupt the young, get them away from religion. Get them interested in sex. Make them superficial, destroy their ruggedness.

B. Get control of all means of publicity and thereby:
1. Get people's mind off their government by focusing their attention on athletics, sexy books, and plays and other trivialities.
2. Divide the people into hostile groups by constantly harping on controversial matters of no importance.
3. Destroy the people's faith in their natural leaders by holding the latter up to contempt, ridicule, and obloquy.
4. Always preach true democracy but seize power as fast and as ruthlessly as possible.
5. By encouraging government extravagance, destroy its credit, produce fear of inflation with rising prices and general discontent.
6. Foment unnecessary strikes in vital industries, encourage civil disorders, and foster a lenient and soft attitude on the part of government toward such disorders.
7. By specious argument cause the breakdown of the old moral virtues: honesty, sobriety, continence, faith in the pledged word, ruggedness.

C. Cause the registration of all firearms on some pretext, with a view of confiscating them and leaving the population helpless.

THE COMMUNIST TAKEOVER OF AMERICA

45 Declared Goals

Communist Goals (1963) Congressional Record--Appendix, pp. A34-A35 January 10, 1963

Current Communist Goals EXTENSION OF REMARKS OF HON. A. S. HERLONG, JR. OF FLORIDA IN THE HOUSE OF REPRESENTATIVES Thursday, January 10, 1963 .

Mr. HERLONG. Mr. Speaker, Mrs. Patricia Nordman of De Land, Fla., is an ardent and articulate opponent of communism, and until recently published the *De Land Courier*, which she dedicated to the purpose of alerting the public to the dangers of communism in America.

At Mrs. Nordman's request, I include in the RECORD, under unanimous consent, the following "Current Communist Goals," which she identifies as an excerpt from "The Naked Communist," by Cleon Skousen:

[From "The Naked Communist," by Cleon Skousen]

1. U.S. acceptance of coexistence as the only alternative to atomic war.
2. U.S. willingness to capitulate in preference to engaging in atomic war.

3. Develop the illusion that total disarmament [by] the United States would be a demonstration of moral strength.

4. Permit free trade between all nations regardless of Communist affiliation and regardless of whether or not items could be used for war.

5. Extension of long-term loans to Russia and Soviet satellites.

6. Provide American aid to all nations regardless of Communist domination.

7. Grant recognition of Red China. Admission of Red China to the U.N.

8. Set up East and West Germany as separate states in spite of Khrushchev's promise in 1955 to settle the German question by free elections under supervision of the U.N.

9. Prolong the conferences to ban atomic tests because the United States has agreed to suspend tests as long as negotiations are in progress.

10. Allow all Soviet satellites individual representation in the U.N.

11. Promote the U.N. as the only hope for mankind. If its charter is rewritten, demand that it be set up as a one-world government with its own independent armed forces. (Some Communist leaders believe the world can be taken over as easily by the U.N. as by Moscow. Sometimes these two centers compete with each other as they are now doing in the Congo.)

12. Resist any attempt to outlaw the Communist Party.

13. Do away with all loyalty oaths.

14. Continue giving Russia access to the U.S. Patent Office.

15. Capture one or both of the political parties in the United States.

16. Use technical decisions of the courts to weaken

basic American institutions by claiming their activities violate civil rights.

17. Get control of the schools. Use them as transmission belts for socialism and current Communist propaganda. Soften the curriculum. Get control of teachers' associations. Put the party line in textbooks.

18. Gain control of all student newspapers.

19. Use student riots to foment public protests against programs or organizations which are under Communist attack.

20. Infiltrate the press. Get control of book-review assignments, editorial writing, policy-making positions.

21. Gain control of key positions in radio, TV, and motion pictures.

22. Continue discrediting American culture by degrading all forms of artistic expression. An American Communist cell was told to "eliminate all good sculpture from parks and buildings, substitute shapeless, awkward and meaningless forms."

23. Control art critics and directors of art museums. "Our plan is to promote ugliness, repulsive, meaningless art."

24. Eliminate all laws governing obscenity by calling them "censorship" and a violation of free speech and free press.

25. Break down cultural standards of morality by promoting pornography and obscenity in books, magazines, motion pictures, radio, and TV.

26. Present homosexuality, degeneracy and promiscuity as "normal, natural, healthy."

27. Infiltrate the churches and replace revealed religion with "social" religion. Discredit the Bible and emphasize the need for intellectual maturity, which does not need a "religious crutch."

28. Eliminate prayer or any phase of religious expression in the schools on the ground that it violates the principle of "separation of church and state."
29. Discredit the American Constitution by calling it inadequate, old-fashioned, out of step with modern needs, a hindrance to cooperation between nations on a worldwide basis.
30. Discredit the American Founding Fathers. Present them as selfish aristocrats who had no concern for the "common man."
31. Belittle all forms of American culture and discourage the teaching of American history on the ground that it was only a minor part of the "big picture." Give more emphasis to Russian history since the Communists took over.
32. Support any socialist movement to give centralized control over any part of the culture—education, social agencies, welfare programs, mental health clinics, etc.
33. Eliminate all laws or procedures which interfere with the operation of the Communist apparatus.
34. Eliminate the House Committee on Un-American Activities.
35. Discredit and eventually dismantle the FBI.
36. Infiltrate and gain control of more unions.
37. Infiltrate and gain control of big business.
38. Transfer some of the powers of arrest from the police to social agencies. Treat all behavioral problems as psychiatric disorders which no one but psychiatrists can understand [or treat].
39. Dominate the psychiatric profession and use mental health laws as a means of gaining coercive control over those who oppose Communist goals.
40. Discredit the family as an institution. Encourage promiscuity and easy divorce.

41. Emphasize the need to raise children away from the negative influence of parents. Attribute prejudices, mental blocks and retarding of children to suppressive influence of parents.

42. Create the impression that violence and insurrection are legitimate aspects of the American tradition; that students and special-interest groups should rise up and use ["]united force ["] to solve economic, political or social problems.

43. Overthrow all colonial governments before native populations are ready for self-government.

44. Internationalize the Panama Canal.

45. Repeal the Connally reservation so the United States cannot prevent the World Court from seizing jurisdiction [over domestic problems. Give the World Court jurisdiction] over nations and individuals alike.

Sources are listed below.

Microfilm: California State University at San Jose Clark Library, Government Floor Phone (408) 924-2770 Microfilm Call Number: J 11.R5

Congressional Record, Vol. 109 88th Congress, 1st Session Appendix Pages A1–A2842 Jan. 9-May 7, 1963 Reel 12

KING SOLOMON
REFUTES COMMUNISM

"My son, if sinners entice thee, consent thou not. If they say, Come with us, let us lay wait for blood, let us lurk privily for the innocent without cause: Let us swallow them up alive as the grave; and whole, as those that go down into the pit: We shall find all precious substance, we shall fill our houses with spoil: Cast in thy lot among us; let us all have one purse: My son, walk not thou in the way with them; refrain thy foot from their path: For their feet run to evil, and make haste to shed blood. Surely in vain the net is spread in the sight of any bird. And they lay wait for their *own* blood; they lurk privily for their *own* lives. So *are* the ways of every one that is greedy of gain; *which* taketh away the life of the owners thereof."

—*King Solomon*
Proverbs 1:10-19, KJV

ABOUT THE AUTHOR

CHAPLAIN (MAJOR) JAMES F. LINZEY, ARNG (RET.) is a retired United States Army Chaplain, having served a combined total of nearly twenty-four years of active duty and reserve duty. Jim began his military career in the United States Air Force on November 5, 1985. On January 4, 1998, he left the Air Force to join the Army. Among Jim's assignments were tours of duty at Maxwell Air Force Base, Montgomery, Alabama, where he attended Air University. Among many subjects, he focused his studies on Leadership Awareness, Team Awareness and Team Leadership. Among the Professional Military Education schools and courses he attended were the Air Force Officers' Orientation Course, the Chaplains Officers' Basic Course, the Chaplains Officers' Advanced Course, the Squadron Officers' School, the Combined Arms and Services Staff School, and the Command and General Staff College.

Military assignments over his twenty-four-year career include Command Chaplain, 5035th Garrison Support Unit, Fort Bliss, Texas; Command Chaplain, Cluster III, Operation Noble Eagle II, White Sands Missile Range, New Mexico, under the Department of Homeland

Security; and Chaplain for the Officer Candidate School at Fort Mead, South Dakota. In the course of his career, Jim trained military personnel in principles and practices of character-based leadership in Joint-Military Leadership Training at the Armed Forces Staff College and aboard the USS *Briscoe* at the Naval Air Station, Norfolk, Virginia, and in the Quartermaster's Officers' Basic Course and Non-commissioned Officers seminars at Fort Lee, Virginia. Jim applied his training while serving on the Leadership Panel at the United States Army Cadet Command's Leader's Training Course at Fort Knox, Kentucky, as its first full-time chaplain. Jim retired from the U.S. Army on June 29, 2009 with an Honorable Discharge at the rank of Major.

Jim attended the Billy Graham School of Evangelism in Ashville, North Carolina. He received a Bachelor of Arts degree from Vanguard University of Southern California, Costa Mesa, California; a Master of Divinity degree from Fuller Theological Seminary, Pasadena, California; and a Doctor of Divinity degree from Kingsway Theological Seminary, Des Moines, Iowa.

Other appearances, including media consist of ABC News, CBS News, CNN News, the Christian Broadcasting Network and the *Glenn Beck Show*. He was a guest on Daystar Television Network, God's Learning Channel, SON Broadcasting Network and Trinity Broadcasting Network. Jim hosted his own television series, which aired on various networks around the world. He also served as a missionary and conducted evangelistic crusades. He supports missions projects in Mexico, the Philippines, India and Africa.

Jim is listed in *Who's Who in America, Who's Who in the World,* the *International Centre of Biography in Cambridge, England*, and *2000 Intellectuals of the 21st Century.*